The World According to
Denise

ILLUSTRATED BY: Denise Chevalier

denise expounds on... ETIQUETTE

When dinner guests ask me if they can "bring anything," I generally say, "Sure... Dinner."

Never ask another woman her age. She might be a month younger than you...
... and you'd have to hate her forever.

Most people send "Thank-You" notes.
I prefer the more appropriate "Thank-me" notes.

On a first date in a fancy restaurant, remember: Always order the most expensive thing on the menu.

This also applies to all following dates.

Shrimp Salad... $9.75
Chateau Briand... $23.00
Quiche lorraine... $10.50
Red Snapper... $16.50
Oysters..... $19.75
   with pearls... $3500.00

Chocolate Mousse
   $4.00
Raspberry Torte
   $2.75

Never speak ill of another person when their back is turned.
MEOW
Wait until they've actually left the room.

You know what I always say...
Better late than pregnant.
TIC TIC
TIC
TAP
TAP
TAP

denise faces facts about... FASHION

Some women are obsessed with their clothes. I think that's narrow-minded and shallow.
What about hair and nails?

If it weren't for stop lights, I'd never get my makeup on.

13

I was walking past this little boutique last week and caught a glimpse of something really cute...

...my reflection.

I can't help but feel sorry for those less fortunate...

CLINK

I ♥ my
typewriter

...flat-chested women, for example.

17

A friend is someone who calms you in times of crisis, supports you in times of trial, and hates you when you look better in a swimsuit.

Some people think they can make their problems disappear by spending a little money.

That's not true at all... you have to spend a lot of money.

20

Some people think they can make their problems disappear by spending a little money.

That's not true at all... you have to spend a lot of money.

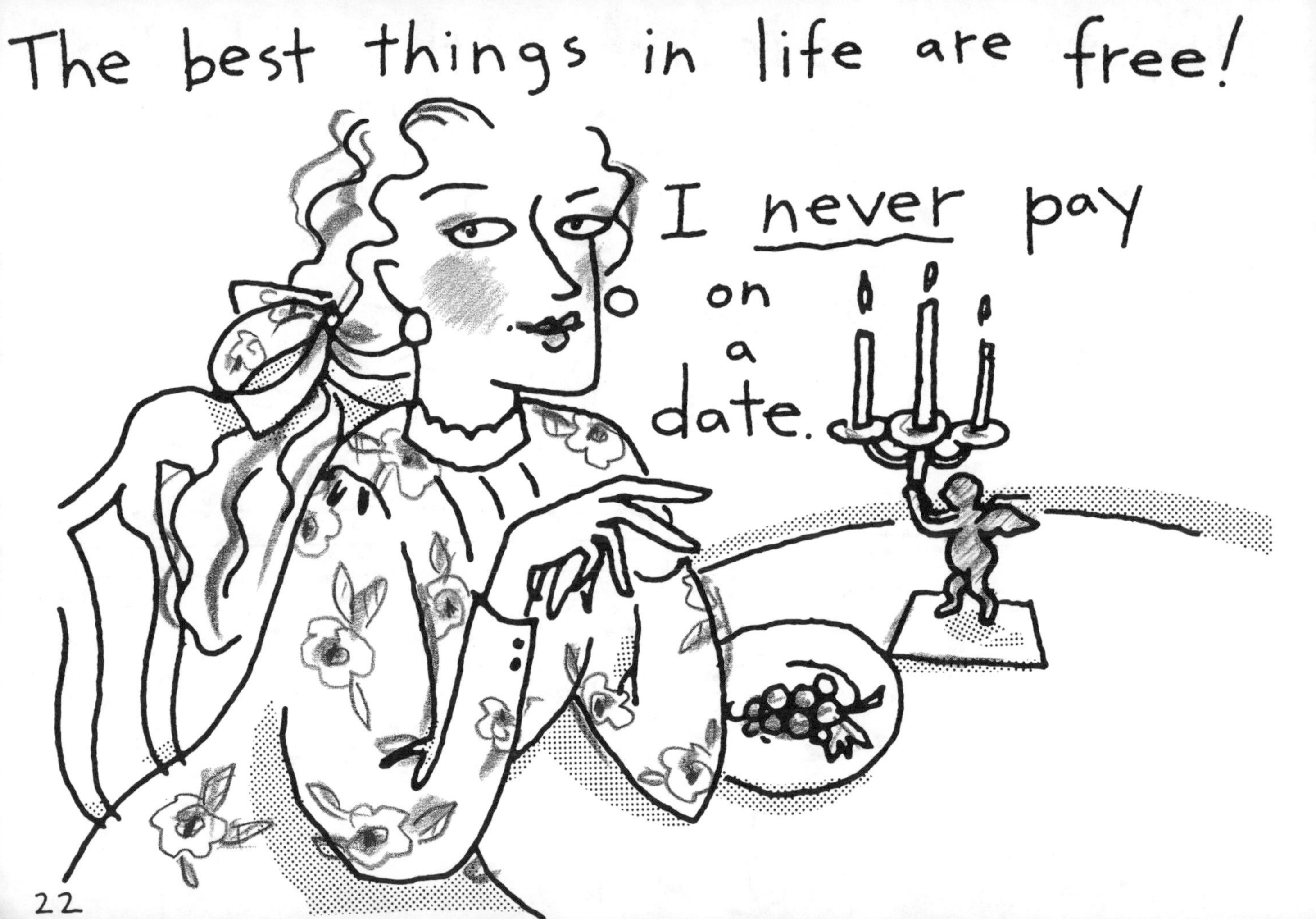
The best things in life are free!
I never pay
on a date.

When I'm feeling stressed, I tend to withdraw a lot
... then I spend it all on clothes.

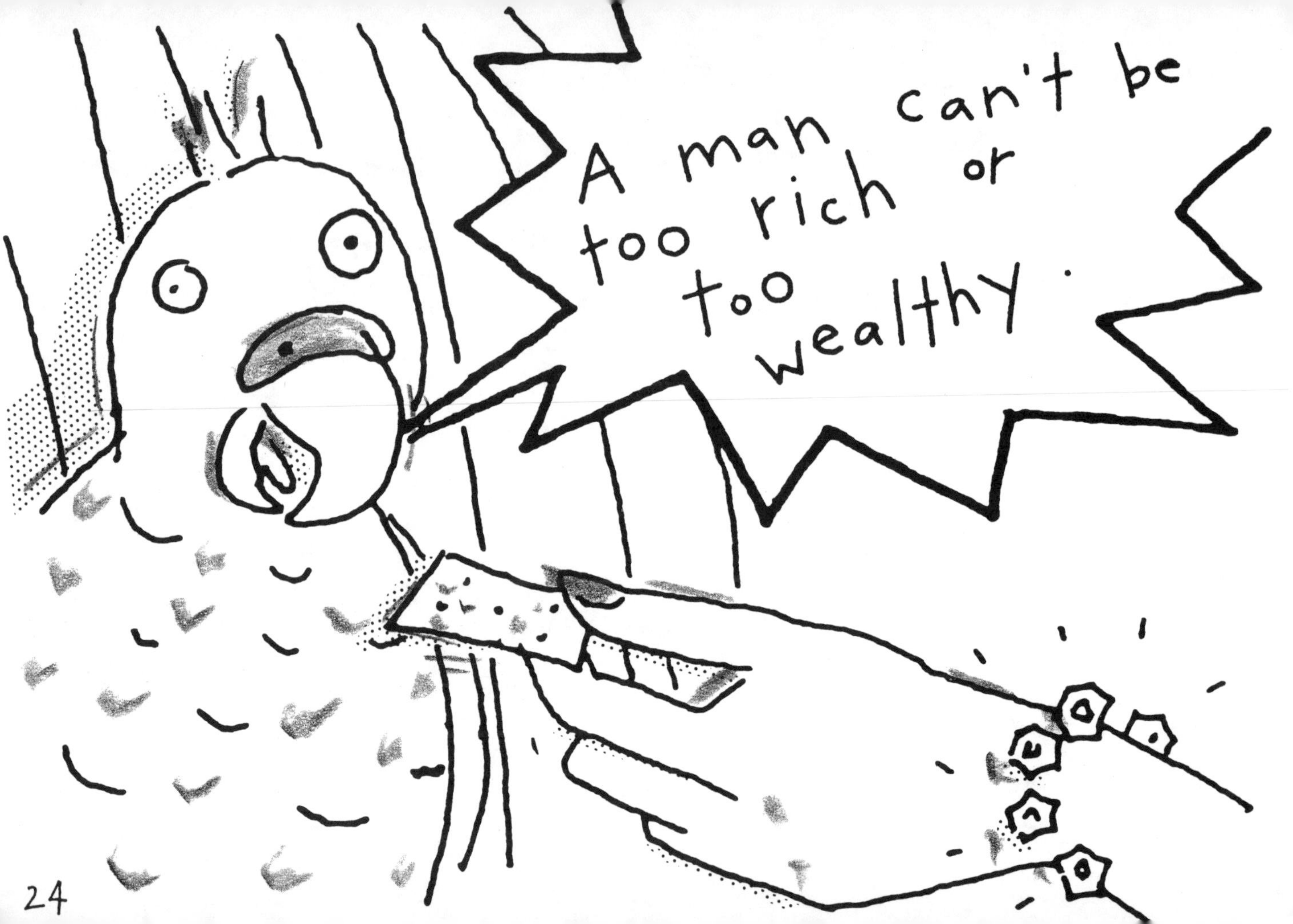
A man can't be too rich or too wealthy.

Little things
mean a lot...

...especially if they're expensive
little things.

25

I spoke to an accountant about my financial prospects. It was horrifying!
Accountants are so boring!

There's more to life than making money.

There's marrying it and spending it.

It's a good idea to have something put away for a rainy day.

I have two bottles of wine, some candles. and a book of massage.

28

denise holds forth on...

HEALTH

and

EXERCISE

30 '' 140 '' 15

29

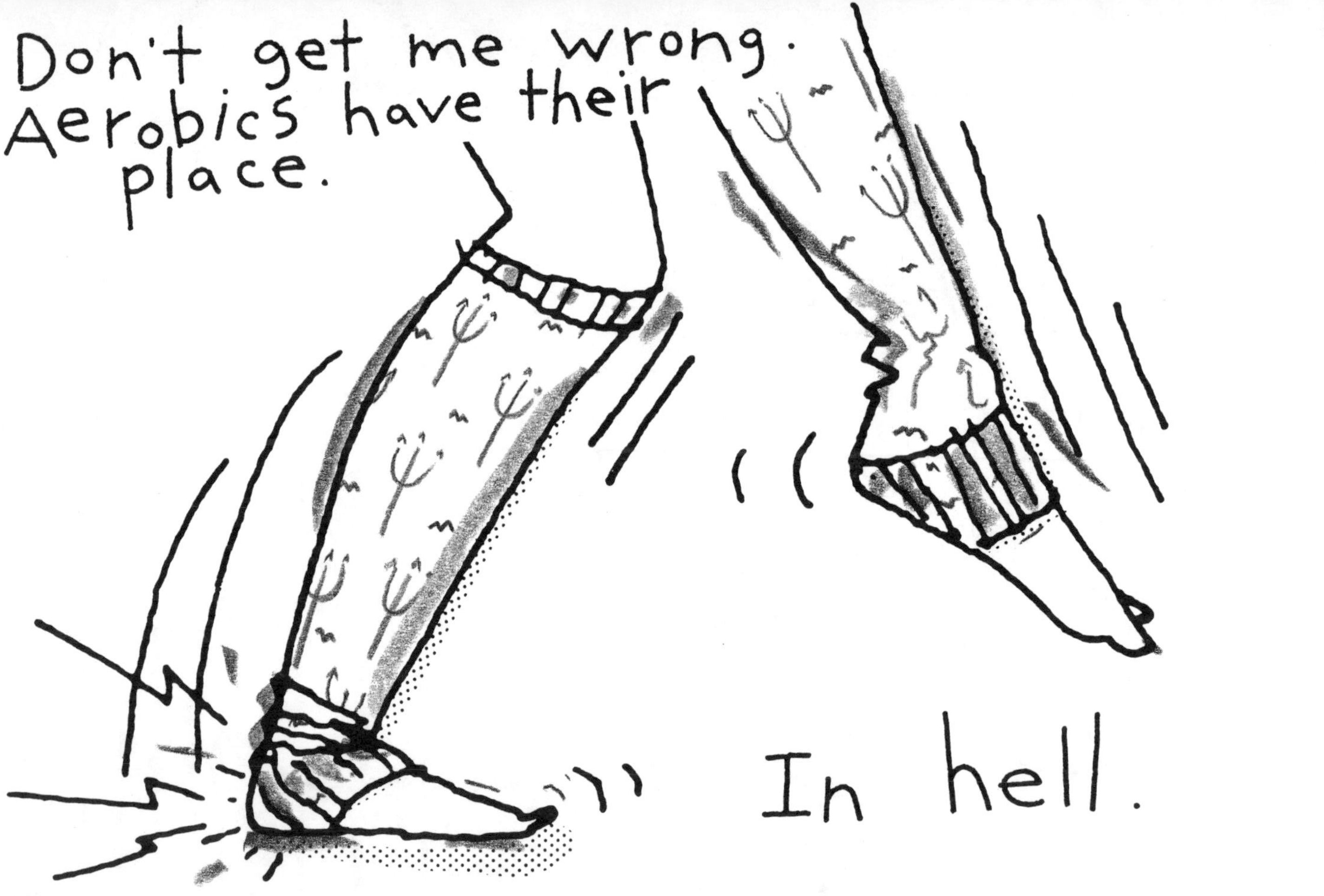

Don't get me wrong. Aerobics have their place.
In hell.

I get enough exercise just pushing my credit limit.

There's only one occasion when I'd consider going camping.

But hell will probably never get that cold.

Things to consider before joining a health spa: You could improve your body; you could meet new, interesting people; you could have better health.

Of course, you could also muss your $85 perm.

33

With sensible diet
and exercise
you can improve
your heart rate,
lower your
blood pressure...

...and get a
smaller waist
than any of your friends.

34

Cycling is a great way to exercise and see breathtaking scenery...

...as long as I'm riding behind a gorgeous guy in those tight black shorts.

35

With hard work and dedication, a woman can achieve the highest of all goals....
... a perfect tan.

There's nothing quite like sitting in a hot tub after a massage and sauna with a hot toddy following an invigorating day...

...of shopping in the chalet gift shop.

I love water sports!

Bubble bath polo, hot tub keep away, shower twister...

Jenise's feelings on...

Food

39

The only two things in life that really matter are chocolate...
... and I can't remember the other one.

If a guy says it's "Dutch treat," he'd better mean he's taking me to Copenhagen.

You're never too old to learn.

For example, I've just learned to say "Dessert menu, please!" in yet another language.

42

Mom taught me everything I know about cooking: "Get rich and hire somebody."

I get a little misty just thinking about it.

43

Nothin' says lovin' like something from Chez Pierre's oven!

44

I don't know why they call it health food.
Makes me sick just to look at it.

What could be more enjoyable than a barbecue in the great outdoors?

Well, how about getting a really bad perm in an ugly flowered smock while listening to country and western music?

Denise lectures on...
Love
and
ROMANCE

47

I get tired of the same old lines:
"Take my car! My house! My inheritance! It's all yours..."
"...Just say you'll be mine!"

Nothing impresses me more than a man who writes a tender love poem and leaves it for me...
...under the windshield wiper of a brand-new sports car.

Remember, blind dates are people, too.

when you shatter their pitiful lives with your rejection, do it gently.

52

I blame a lot of my moodiness on P.M.S.
women who still believe men have a clue... Today on vivaldo!
Pure Male Stupidity.

As a concerned citizen, I like to do my part to protect the environment.
Every few weeks, I recycle boyfriends.

Remember, there's more to romance than "sex".

unless, of course, you're a "man".

53

The sum total
of all useful
functions
performed
by men:

parallel
parking,

killing
bugs,

sex.

Oh well,
two and a-half out of three's not bad.

I just love parties... the stimulating conversations, the fascinating small talk, the witty jokes.

But enough about my contributions.

56

My idea of "roughing it" is a room service menu with a less-than-adequate wine list.

57

Over the years, I've developed an appreciation of the fine Arts.
And the wonderful Bills.
And the fabulous Erics.
And the gorgeous Brians.
And the...

I love to get out in nature at the mercy of the elements... the sun, the wind...
...that's why I occasionally put the top down on my Porsche.

A cruise is a good opportunity to get away from it all, see exciting new locations, and, best of all...
... look better than a whole new group of people.

61

Often you can forget the cares of the world by settling back with a good work of fiction...
TWENTY DAYS TO A PERFECT BODY,
for example.

denise waxes witty on...

WORK and *Career*

63

Office life is full of vicious gossip, constant backbiting, and ego-shattering confrontations.

Isn't it great!

64

I have a policy about dating men at work:
They have to make at least $80 thousand a year.

On a drowsy morning, nothing gets you going like a freshly brewed cup of coffee.

Especially if it's handed to you by a tall, single guy from accounting whose taut muscles stretch the rich fabric of his tailored shirt.

Office parties are great opportunities to make new friends from other departments, increase valuable business contacts...

...and viciously ridicule coworkers' wives

what your are wearing.

67

I always make sure to put in a full 40 hours of hard work.
Next year I may try for 45.

I'm always willing to
go the extra mile
at
work.

Especially if they're
out of chocolate in the
vending machine on my floor.

My boss is limiting us to one personal phone call a day which I think is really unfair.
I mean, who am I going to talk to for eight hours straight?

WRITTEN BY: Lee Ann Ahern, Chris Brethwaite, Bill Bridgeman, Bill Gray, Allyson Jones, Kevin Kinzer, Mark Oatman, Scott Oppenheimer, Dan Taylor, Rich Warwick and Myra Zirkle.